THE TATER TOT CASSEROLE COOKBOOK

BY KERRIE MCLOUGHLIN

ISBN-13: 978-1519464484

ISBN-10: 1519464487

DEDICATION

This book is dedicated to Jordan McGarrigle, who we met when she was 11 years old. She was first a Mother's Helper, then a babysitter, and soon became a trusted friend and part of the family. She was instrumental in making this cookbook happen ... helping to come up with ideas and trying the new creations as we cooked them together with all my kids running around us.

We love you, Jordan, and wish you the best as you embark on your college journey and on the rest of your life!

CONTENTS

DESSERTS

ACKNOWLEDGMENTS

Thank you to my husband Aron, my best friend, for everything you do to love and support me, including always cooking on the weekends!

There aren't words to express what my kids, Joel, Michael, Callie, Eva, and Samuel, mean to me and how much I love being home with them every day. Thank you for sleeping late while I worked on this book!

Thank you to Julia, for making me your Confirmation sponsor and being like a sister to my kids.

Thank you to my parents for giving me a rockin' childhood with plenty of time built in for reading and writing.

Thank you to my in-laws for loving me like one of your own.

Thank you to my friends, old and new, and I am blessed that there are too many to name.

Thank you to my neighbors, because when our kids are all playing together, I sneak in writing time ☺

And the biggest thanks goes to God, for all the great works He has done in my life and continues to do!

WHY TATER TOT CASSEROLE AND WHY A NEW VERSION OF THE BOOK?

Who doesn't love a good tater tot casserole? It's a classic meat-and-potatoes meal that's easy, cheap, and customizable. You can make tater tot casserole in so many different ways depending on your own likes and tastes and those of your family. It's such a versatile dish, and there is just so much to love about this meal, like:

- It tastes great.
- You can make it gluten-free or to meet other dietary specifications or restrictions.
- You can make it healthy or really pile on the full-fat cheese.

- Kids and adults both love it.
- It's easy to make.
- It's fast to make.
- It's cheap to make.
- It's a meat-and-potatoes meal so guys dig it.
- It's a comfort food.
- It feeds many, so ...
- It is the perfect dish to take to a potluck.
- It is the perfect dish to take to a new mom.
- It is the perfect dish to take to a sick person.
- It's perfect for those who don't enjoy cooking.
- It's wonderful for those who work all day and need something fast.
- It's a great freezer meal.
- It's a great leftover meal.
- It's awesome for the older generations, who are so sick of cooking that they are now eating out all the time.

Lately you can also find onion-flavored tater tots, which would be a great replacement for some of the plain tater tots in this cookbook. Also, be sure to try whipping up a recipe like Turkey Tater Tot Casserole or the Basic version using sweet potato tots!

I updated this book from the original Kindle ebook version, first, because I wanted to get it into a print version so I could have a copy to gift to friends, family, neighbors, and other loved ones. I wanted it to be available to purchase for those who like to have a physical cookbook. My kids should also have copies for when they are on their own!

I'm also updating the book because I read my reviews on Amazon and customers were wanting exact measurements (sorry, it's my first cookbook, but I've made it right!). I want my readers to be happy, so I've made improvements! I also made the font large so it's easy to read for everyone ☺

**I have added a special tater tot recipe (Fully

Loaded!) and a bunch more dessert recipes. I also wanted to give a little personal introduction to each recipe to make it more fun. *Amazon dictates the minimum price, which was going to be $17 with just a few color recipe photos, so I took out photos and instead you get a less expensive cookbook AND you can get the Kindle version for free (tons of pictures there because past customers asked for them!).*

I hope you enjoy reading and cooking/baking from this new version as much as I enjoyed writing it!

TATER TOT CASSEROLE TIPS

Here's the main question of this entire e-cookbook: Do you like your tots crispy or soft?

Most of the recipes in this cookbook call for putting the evaporated milk and soups on TOP of the tots. It makes for a great meat and potatoes meal in most cases. If you prefer your tots crispy, though, just put the soups/milk on the bottom, top with tots, then cheese, then bake, which is how my family likes this tasty dish! Here are some more tips:

- When a recipe calls for ground beef, feel free to use ground turkey or even sausage instead if you wish.

- White meat ground turkey or chicken is better if you're watching your health or weight.

- I have had great luck in making a couple of these recipes ahead of time and putting them in the freezer. Just take one out in the morning and it should be thawed enough to pop in the oven about an hour before dinner. Also great if you are baking ahead to share a meal with a new mom or someone who is sick and their family needs meals.

- Add any veggie you like to any of the recipes or serve with something on the side like carrot sticks, applesauce, canned or fresh fruit salad, Jell-O with fruit in it, or canned, frozen, or fresh veggies.

- Feel free to substitute any other cream of soup if you prefer another kind.

- If you dig something like onions or peppers, add them by all means! Onions make me toot after I get a stomach-ache and I can't handle the texture of mushrooms (like snails!), so I leave them out.

- If you don't need a full 9 x 13" pan because there are only one or two people in your household, the recipes are usually easy to cut in half. Or you can make a full pan and freeze half immediately or use it for a meal swap! If you have a very large family, just double it!

TATER TOT FUNNIES

One night while trying to fall asleep, my husband and I came up with some goofy names for the classic tater tot.

- ★ Tater thumbs
- ★ Tater toes
- ★ Tater tweets
- ★ Tater poops
- ★ Tater buns
- ★ Tater dots
- ★ Tater spots
- ★ Tater cylinders
- ★ Tater cans
- ★ Tater babies

★ Laura Piawlock sent in this one to me: Children of Potato

★ Your idea here

Send your suggestions to me via email at mommykerrie@yahoo.com for the next edition of the book!

MEAL PLANNING BASICS

Look, I know you can't eat tater tot casserole every day of the year. That would get boring for sure. Even my family gets sick of it when I make it weekly so I have to come up with other things to make.

If you're anything like me, by the time 5 p.m. rolls around, you don't know what's for dinner. You scramble around the pantry and the fridge looking for something, ANYTHING, to put together fast. Then maybe you hit Facebook and let your friends know that you need ideas for dinner and that you have these four ingredients in your home. They probably will explain to you that spaghetti sauce, cream of chicken soup, yogurt, and tuna will *never* be friends. So you give up and call one of your pals, either the pizza or the Chinese food delivery guy.

I am here to tell you that dinner doesn't have to be a stressful, last-minute chore. I finally figured out a system for making it easy, and it only requires a little bit of planning and then checking out your meal plan each morning. The bonus is that you'll save money both by not eating out as a last resort *and* by using items you already have in your pantry, freezer and fridge. Below is a fairly quick strategy to use when you're feeling frazzled about mealtimes. Give it a try!

First, take into account the season. What's in season, what's fresh, what's cheap, what do you love to eat when it's around only for a short time? For me, I like to eat much lighter in the summertime and fill up on berries, watermelon, and other fruit as sides for meals rather than canned or frozen veggies.

Second, think about what everyone in your household likes and eats without too much of a struggle. If you have kids, what could they help make? I make very basic, easy meals, but my husband is pretty much a gourmet cook, so I need to plan at least one meal on the weekend for him to make the way he likes. Haul out those recipe cards and cookbooks and hit Pinterest or your favorite recipe sites if you are drawing a total blank.

The third step is to figure out what you already have in the house so you can build around that. Go to the pantry and fridge and freezer and write everything down if you need to. Send the kids to the computer to look up sites where they can put in their favorite ingredients and come up with a recipe. Teach them how to make a balanced meal and how they could substitute strawberries for a veggie one night.

The fourth step is to check out your local grocery store ads and also figure out what coupons you have around (I also like to use the Ibotta app for cash-back rebates once you hit $20 in earned credits). Don't use a coupon just because you have one. Use it if it meets the needs of your meal plan, or you could always buy the coupon item and plan a meal around that.

The fifth step is to set up your plan, using your calendar and a system for listing the meals and ingredients to shop for. I like to use an Excel spreadsheet so I can add different sheets for different meal plans and for tallying up approximate grocery costs. One sheet has a two-week meal plan with the date down one column, the day of the week down the next and the meal down the final, largest column. My sheet only has dinners on it, but you can also add breakfasts and lunches if you wish, which is a great idea so you don't have to think as much! Since my family is home all day, we generally have leftovers for lunch or else PB&J sandwiches with fruit or something like mac 'n cheese with hot dogs and fruit. For breakfast, I just keep things stocked like cereal, oatmeal, yogurt, fruit, eggs, and frozen sausage, hash browns, and waffles.

Work with your calendar close by and take into account nights over the next two weeks (you may want to only meal plan for one week) you might have leftovers on hand, nights you have to make something in a hurry or put something in the slow cooker in the morning, nights you have company over or when you are going out. Of course, you can even build in a night or two for delivery or eating out! Consider doubling ingredients and adding some foil pans to your shopping list so you can easily double a recipe on any given night and put one in the freezer or share it.

Once the plan is in place, print it out and then set up a separate sheet for your grocery list. Working off of your meal plan, type in grocery items. Some people like to grocery shop with their list set up by section of the store; I like to put items in alphabetical order.

I also put an approximate cost of what I'm buying so I know what to expect at checkout and know if I'm staying within my grocery budget.

Consult your plan daily and take out what you'll need for dinner in the morning. For instance, if you want to make a quick boxed meal, take out the hamburger so it'll thaw by the time you want to put the meal together. If you're grilling out, make sure your steaks are out of the freezer in time to be grill-ready.

If you want to kick it up a notch and REALLY be prepared for mealtime without having to do the work every night, consider spending a weekend day cooking for an entire month. You basically spend a few hours on the weekend cooking and freezing meals that you can eat for the entire next week (or longer). I personally haven't had time to do this in years but I plan to do it soon because I remember how great it was to have a freezer stocked full of meals that only needed to be thawed in the morning and were mostly ready to go at night.

Tip: If you know you'll be gone all day tomorrow, fill your slow cooker tonight with something simple like pork chops with some potatoes, veggies, and a can of soup. Store it in the fridge overnight, then in the morning just plug in the slow cooker and turn it on so you'll have a hearty dinner when you get home. OR ... cook the meat for tacos in advance, so all you have to do is heat it up and get the fixins on the table.

TATER TOT CASSEROLE RECIPES (35)

I can't wait for you to try some of these recipes! It is my sincere hope that you find some new favorite meals for yourself, for your family, for your friends … and something easy and fun to take to the next potluck that comes up, to a friend who has just had a baby, or to someone in need!

ASPARAGUS CHICKEN

If you love asparagus, you'll love this version of tater tot casserole! It's a little healthier because it's made with chicken and it's got a veggie in it, so you've got your mealtime bases covered. Feel free to pre-boil or oven-roast some fresh asparagus instead of using canned.

3 boneless skinless chicken breasts
Olive oil; salt and pepper
1 15-ounce can asparagus pieces
2 pounds frozen tater tots
1 12-ounce can evaporated milk
1 10.5-ounce can cream of asparagus soup
1 10.5-ounce can cream of chicken soup
2 cups Monterey Jack cheese

1. Preheat oven to 350 degrees and spray the bottom of a 9 x 13" pan with cooking spray.
2. Put about 2 T. olive oil in a skillet warmed on medium heat.
3. Cut chicken into bite-size pieces, then put pieces in the pan. Toss a little salt and pepper

on the chicken and cook until it is no longer pink inside.

4. Place chicken in the bottom of the sprayed 9 x 13" pan, juice and all.

5. Drain the can of asparagus pieces and spoon over the chicken.

6. Dump the bag of tater tots over the chicken and asparagus, and arrange them so the chicken is covered.

7. In a bowl, mix the evaporated milk and soups. Pour mixture evenly over the top of the tater tots.

8. Top with cheese.

9. Bake uncovered for about 30 minutes.

10. Take out of the oven and let cool for a few minutes before serving.

Bacon Cheeseburger

I grew up loving bacon cheeseburger pizza, so this is one of my favorite tater tot casserole variations. It takes a little longer to make since you have to fry the bacon up first, but it's totally worth it. Skip the onions if you're going to be kissing anybody!

½ pound bacon, cooked crispy
1 ½ pounds ground beef
½ cup chopped onions
2 pounds frozen tater tots
2 10.5-ounce cans cheddar cheese soup
1 cup shredded cheddar cheese
1 12-ounce can evaporated milk
1 cup shredded mozzarella cheese

1. Preheat oven to 350 degrees and spray the bottom of a 9 x 13" pan with cooking spray.
2. In a skillet, cook bacon on medium heat until crispy, then put it on a couple of paper towels to soak up some of the grease.
3. In the same pan, cook ground beef and chopped onions on medium heat until meat is brown.

Drain the fat, then put meat/onion mixture in the bottom of the sprayed 9 x 13" pan.

4. Dump the bag of tater tots over the meat and arrange them so the meat is all snuggly and covered up.

5. In a bowl, mix the evaporated milk and soups. Pour mixture evenly over the top of the tater tots.

6. Top with cheeses.

7. Bake uncovered for about 30 minutes.

8. Take out of the oven and let cool for a few minutes before serving.

BACON RANCH

My daughter Eva freaks out over bacon and would sit and eat a whole pound of cooked bacon if I would let her! My oldest son Joel loves Ranch dressing. Together they make the perfect combination!

½ pound bacon, cooked crispy
1 ½ pounds ground beef
¾ cup bacon Ranch salad dressing
2 pounds frozen tater tots
1 12-ounce can evaporated milk
2 10.5-ounce cans cheddar cheese soup
1 cup shredded cheddar cheese
1 cup shredded mozzarella cheese

1. Preheat oven to 350 degrees and spray the bottom of a 9 x 13" pan with cooking spray.
2. In a skillet, cook bacon on medium heat until crispy, then put it on a couple of paper towels to soak up some of the grease. Crumble bacon to save for later.
3. In the same pan, cook ground beef on medium heat until brown. Drain the fat, then put meat in the bottom of the sprayed 9 x 13" pan.

4. Mix salad dressing into the ground beef mixture.

5. Dump the bag of tater tots over the meat mixture and arrange them so the meat is covered.

6. In a bowl, mix the evaporated milk and soups. Pour evenly over the top of the tater tots.

7. Top with cheese.

8. Bake at 350 degrees uncovered for about 30 minutes.

9. Remove from oven and let cool for a few minutes before serving.

BACON SWISS

I just had to put three bacon recipes in this cookbook since we are such a bacon-loving family. Feel free to substitute another favorite soup for the cream of mushroom (I personally can't stand mushrooms so I always use cream of chicken instead!). Top with Swiss cheese and you have a yummy surprise taste!

1 pound bacon, cooked crispy
1 pound ground beef
2 pounds frozen tater tots
1 12-ounce can evaporated milk
2 10.5-ounce cans cream of mushroom soup
10 slices Swiss cheese

1. Preheat oven to 350 degrees and spray the bottom of a 9 x 13" pan with cooking spray.

2. In a skillet, cook bacon on medium heat until crispy, then put it on a couple of paper towels to soak up some of the grease.

3. In the same pan, cook ground beef on medium heat until brown. Drain the fat, then put meat in the bottom of the sprayed 9 x 13" pan.

4. Crumble bacon and save half for later. Add half the bacon to the ground beef mixture in the pan.

5. Dump the bag of tater tots over the meat mixture and arrange them so the meat is covered.

6. In a bowl, mix the evaporated milk and soups. Pour evenly over the top of the tater tots.

7. Bake at 350 degrees uncovered for about 25 minutes.

8. Grab an oven mitt and take pan out of oven. Top with cheese slices and the remaining crispy bacon and put back in the oven for another 5 minutes.

9. Remove from oven and let cool for a few minutes before serving.

BARBIE-Q

My family is from the Midwest ... Kansas City, specifically, where we are certainly famous for our barbecue. I had to do a twist on the name since I have two girls, Eva and Callie, who play with Barbies ☺

1 ½ pounds ground beef
1 ½ cups KC Masterpiece BBQ sauce
2 pounds frozen tater tots
1 12-ounce can evaporated milk
1 10.5-ounce can cream of chicken soup
1 10.5-ounce can cheddar cheese soup
1 cup shredded cheddar cheese
1 cup shredded mozzarella cheese

1. Preheat oven to 350 degrees and spray the bottom of a 9 x 13" pan with cooking spray.
2. In a skillet, cook ground beef on medium heat until brown. Drain the fat, then put meat in the bottom of the sprayed 9 x 13" pan.
3. Add barbecue sauce to the ground beef and mix together.
4. Dump the bag of tater tots over the meat and arrange them so the meat is covered.

5. In a bowl, mix the evaporated milk and soups. Pour evenly over the top of the tater tots.

6. Top with cheese.

7. Bake at 350 degrees uncovered for about 30 minutes.

8. Take out of the oven and let cool for a few minutes before serving.

BASIC

This is the recipe that got me started on my love of tater tot casserole and the ease of it and the popularity of it among everyone I met! Just 5 simple ingredients plus some spices to taste and you're all set. You can serve a veggie on the side or toss one in the basic recipe when you put in the ground beef bottom layer.

1 ½ pounds ground beef
2 tsp. garlic salt
2 tsp. onion powder
2 pounds frozen tater tots
1 12-ounce can evaporated milk
2 10.5-ounce cans cream of chicken soup
2 cups shredded cheddar cheese

1. Preheat oven to 350 degrees and spray the bottom of a 9 x 13" pan with cooking spray.
2. In a skillet, cook ground beef on medium heat until brown. Drain the fat and put meat back in skillet.

3. Mix in onion powder and garlic salt, then put mixture in the bottom of the sprayed 9 x 13" pan.

4. Dump out the bag of tater tots over the meat and arrange them so the meat is covered.

5. In a bowl, mix the evaporated milk and soups. Pour evenly over the top of the tater tots.

6. Top with cheese.

7. Bake uncovered for about 30 minutes.

8. Take out of the oven and let cool for a few minutes before serving.

BREAKFAST

Why should tater tot casserole just be for dinner? Why not add some breakfast sausage and eggs to make it a breakfast meal? Another thing I like to do is use the leftovers of the Basic recipe: toss it all in a skillet, add some already-scrambled eggs and more cheese, and you have breakfast repurposed. Maybe even add some Lawry's season salt!

1 ½ pounds ground breakfast sausage
2 pounds frozen tater tots
12 eggs
½ cup milk
2 cups shredded cheddar cheese
Salt and pepper to taste

1. Preheat oven to 350 degrees and spray the bottom of a 9 x 13" pan with cooking spray.
2. In a skillet, cook sausage on medium heat until done. Drain the fat and put sausage in the bottom of the sprayed 9 x 13" pan.
3. Dump out the bag of tater tots over the sausage and arrange them so the meat is covered.

4. In a bowl, mix the eggs, milk, salt, and pepper. Pour evenly over the top of the tater tots.

5. Top with cheese.

6. Bake at 350 degrees uncovered for about 1 hour.

7. Take out of the oven and let cool for a few minutes before serving.

BROCCOLI TURKEY

My kids are very strange and they love broccoli; always have. Of course, this means I had to come up with a special recipe incorporating a veggie into the tater tot casserole! Enjoy!

2 cups diced turkey or 1 ½ pounds white meat
   ground turkey
2 tsp. onion powder
2 cups frozen broccoli spears, thawed
2 pounds frozen tater tots
1 12-ounce can evaporated milk
1 10.5-ounce can cream of broccoli soup
1 10.5-ounce can cheddar cheese soup
2 cups shredded cheddar cheese

1. Preheat oven to 350 degrees and spray the bottom of a 9 x 13" pan with cooking spray.
2. In a skillet, cook ground turkey or diced turkey on medium heat until brown/warmed.
3. Mix in onion powder and put turkey mixture in the bottom of the sprayed 9 x 13" pan.
4. Chop up broccoli and place on top of turkey.

5. Dump out the bag of tater tots over the turkey and arrange them so the meat is covered.

6. In a bowl, mix the evaporated milk and soups. Pour evenly over the top of the tater tots.

7. Top with cheese.

8. Bake uncovered for about 30 minutes.

9. Take out of the oven and let cool for a few minutes before serving.

Buffalo Bleu Cheese Chicken

My husband is the biggest fan on this concoction since he loves spicy anything (including his wife)! I have to tone it down when I'm first making it and then those in my family who enjoy hot sauce just add to theirs on their plate after they have been served.

2 pounds chicken breasts
Olive oil; salt and pepper
6 T. Louisiana hot sauce
2 pounds frozen tater tots
1 cup crumbled bleu cheese
1 12-ounce can evaporated milk
2 10.5-ounce cans cream of chicken soup

1. Preheat oven to 350 degrees and spray the bottom of a 9 x 13" pan with cooking spray.
2. Put about 2 T. olive oil in a skillet warmed on medium heat.
3. Cut chicken into bite-size pieces, then put pieces in the pan. Toss a little salt and pepper on the chicken and cook until it is no longer pink inside.

4. Salt and pepper the chicken just a smidge.

5. Add 6 T. Louisiana Hot Sauce and stir together in pan. Put chicken in the bottom of the sprayed 9 x 13" pan.

6. Dump out the bag of tater tots over the meat and arrange them so the chicken is covered.

7. Crumble bleu cheese over the top of the tots.

8. In a bowl, mix the evaporated milk and soups. Pour evenly over the top of the tater tots.

9. Bake at 350 degrees uncovered for about 30 minutes.

10. Take out of the oven and let cool for a few minutes before serving.

CHICKEN (SLOW COOKER)

For some reason, I just don't like the taste of chicken that's been boiled in water. It's also a pain for me to cook it in a skillet (pre-cut into small cubes or not). Enter the slow cooker! I just toss some chicken in there and it does the work for me all day. Later on, I just assemble the whole meal and toss it in the oven for a bit!

4 boneless skinless chicken breasts
Salt and pepper
2 pounds frozen tater tots
1 12-ounce can evaporated milk
2 10.5-ounce cans cream of chicken soup
2 cups shredded cheddar cheese

1. Preheat oven to 350 degrees and spray the bottom of a 9 x 13" pan with cooking spray.

2. Put chicken in slow cooker around noon and cook on low for 4 hours and then just leave it in the slow cooker until you're ready for it.

3. When you're ready to make dinner, dice the chicken then put it in the bottom of the sprayed 9 x 13" pan. Save any broth!

4. Sprinkle some salt and pepper over the chicken.

5. Dump out the bag of tater tots over the meat and arrange them so the chicken is covered.

6. In a bowl, mix the evaporated milk, soups, and ½ cup of the chicken broth, or however much you have left. Pour evenly over the top of the tater tots.

7. Top with cheese.

8. Bake at 350 degrees uncovered for about 30 minutes.

9. Take out of the oven and let cool for a few minutes before serving.

CHICKEN ALFREDO

Just like with the Chicken (Slow Cooker) recipe, you can also put this chicken in the slow cooker if you like. Then just take it out when it's all done, chop it up and then assemble as usual. The Alfredo sauce makes it extra creamy and the mozzarella pairs with it perfectly, or try another kind of cheese you love!

3 boneless skinless chicken breasts
2 T. minced garlic; olive oil
2 pounds frozen tater tots
2 15-ounce jars Alfredo sauce
2 cups shredded mozzarella cheese

1. Preheat oven to 350 degrees and spray the bottom of a 9 x 13" pan with cooking spray.

2. Put about 2 T. olive oil in a skillet warmed on medium heat, then add garlic.

3. Cut chicken into bite-size pieces, then put pieces in the skillet. Cook chicken until it's no longer pink inside.

4. Place chicken in the bottom of the sprayed 9 x 13" pan, juice and all.

5. Pour both jars of Alfredo sauce evenly over the top of the tater tots.

6. Dump out the bag of tater tots over the chicken and arrange them so the meat is covered.

7. Top with cheese.

8. Bake at 350 degrees uncovered for about 30 minutes.

9. Take out of the oven and let cool for a few minutes before serving.

* we used Classico 4-cheese Alfredo sauce

CHILI CHEESE

We really get into our Chili Cheese Fritos® around here, so I wondered how that would go over with my lovely tots. Turns out it works out in a VERY yummy manner! If you don't want the ground beef or don't want to make your own chili, feel free to use canned. We are all about easy around here!

1 ½ pounds ground beef
1 1-ounce package chili seasoning, any brand
6 T. water
2 15.5-ounce cans chili beans
Onion powder/garlic powder*
2 pounds frozen tater tots
1 12-ounce can evaporated milk
2 10.5-ounce cans cheddar cheese soup
2 cups shredded cheddar cheese
Sour cream

1. Preheat oven to 350 degrees and spray the bottom of a 9 x 13" pan with cooking spray.
2. In a skillet, cook ground beef on medium heat until brown. Drain the fat and put meat back in skillet.

3. Mix in chili seasoning and water. Add extra onion powder and garlic powder to taste. Put mixture in the bottom of the sprayed 9 x 13" pan.

4. Add chili beans to the baking pan and mix with meat.

5. Dump out the bag of tater tots over the meat and arrange them so the meat is covered.

6. Pour soups evenly over the top of the tater tots.

7. Top with cheese.

8. Bake at 350 degrees uncovered for about 30 minutes.

9. Take out of the oven and let cool for a few minutes before serving.

10. Top each serving with a dollop of sour cream.

* Depending on how you like your chili, you might want to spruce it up with tomatoes, onions, and peppers before transferring to the pan.

CORN

Once my husband was telling a coworker about my tater tot casserole and the guy asked, "Where's the vegetable?" Well, good question, well-meaning dude. That's what inspired me to include cream-style corn and regular corn in this recipe because it's one of my favorite veggies … and there you go! Warning: this is not a light recipe!

1 pound ground beef
1 15-ounce can whole kernel corn, drained
1 15-ounce can cream-style corn
½ cup butter, melted
1 cup sour cream
2 pounds frozen tater tots
2 cups shredded cheddar cheese

1. Preheat oven to 350 degrees and spray the bottom of a 9 x 13" pan with cooking spray.
2. In a skillet, cook ground beef on medium heat until brown. Drain the fat, then put meat in the sprayed 9 x 13" pan.
3. In a bowl, mix corns, butter, and sour cream. Pour over meat.

4. Dump out the bag of tater tots over the meat and arrange them so the meat is covered.

5. Top with cheese.

6. Bake at 350 degrees uncovered for about 30 minutes.

7. Take out of the oven and let cool for a few minutes before serving.

Dairy-Free

I like to be respectful of those who don't or are not able to eat exactly like myself and my family. And, really, it doesn't kill us to try something different. So this one is for my lactose-challenged peeps with a faux "cream-of" soup and minus the cheese.

1 ½ pounds ground beef
2 15-ounce cans green beans, drained
Garlic powder, pepper
1 2-ounce package onion soup mix
Make your own faux "cream of" soup (see below)
2 pounds frozen tater tots

Faux "Cream of" Soup
1 ¼ cups chicken broth
¾ cup almond milk
1/3 cup flour
Dash of each: salt, pepper, garlic powder, onion powder
Pinch of each: basil, oregano

1. Preheat oven to 350 degrees and spray the bottom of a 9 x 13" pan with cooking spray.

2. Put chicken broth with ¼ cup of the almond milk in a saucepan and bring to a low boil.

3. Into the rest of the almond milk, whisk in the flour, dashes, and pinches until smooth.

4. Pour your cold mixture into the saucepan and put the heat on low. Whisk nonstop so you don't get lumpy soup and keep doing that until it's of a "cream of" consistency you like.

5. In a skillet, cook ground beef on medium heat until brown. Drain the fat and put meat back into skillet.

6. Add garlic powder and pepper to taste, then put meat in the sprayed 9 x 13" pan.

7. Add soup mix, green beans, and your faux "cream of" soup mixture to meat in pan.

8. Dump out the bag of tater tots over the meat and arrange them so the meat is covered.

9. Bake uncovered for about 30 minutes.

10. Take out of the oven and let cool for a few minutes before serving.

Extra Creamy

Interesting how this one follows the dairy-free recipe when they are opposites! Sometimes you might need to make a light version of tater tot casserole and sometimes you might want to be naughty ... like when you are taking a dish to a potluck full of skinny people (wink). And sometimes you really are in need of a calorie-laded comfort food for yourself!

1 ½ pounds ground beef
Garlic powder/onion salt
1 brick 1/3 less fat cream cheese
2 pounds frozen tater tots
1 cup mayonnaise
1 12-ounce can evaporated milk
1 10.5-ounce can cream of chicken soup
1 cup shredded mozzarella cheese
1 cup shredded cheddar cheese

1. Preheat oven to 350 degrees and spray the bottom of a 9 x 13" pan with cooking spray.
2. In a skillet, cook ground beef on medium heat until brown. Drain the fat and put meat back in skillet.
3. Mix in garlic powder and onion salt to taste.

4. Stir in cream cheese, then put mixture in the bottom of the sprayed 9 x 13" pan.

5. Dump out the bag of tater tots over the meat/cream cheese and arrange them so the meat is covered.

6. In a bowl, mix mayonnaise, milk and soup. Pour evenly over the top of the tater tots.

7. Top with cheese.

8. Bake uncovered for about 30 minutes.

9. Take out of the oven and let cool for a few minutes before serving.

FISH STICK SURPRISE

So most kids love fish sticks, right? Surprise! This dish has fish sticks all lined up in a row ready to be eaten (perfect Lenten dish!). My son Sam really dug this meal when I made it because he loves fish! As always, feel free to change up the soups and/or cheese.

24 frozen fish sticks, baked
2 pounds frozen tater tots
1 10.5-ounce can cream of chicken soup
1 10.5-ounce can cream of mushroom soup
1 12-ounce can evaporated milk
2 cups shredded cheddar cheese

1. Preheat oven to 350 degrees and spray the bottom of a 9 x 13" pan with cooking spray.
2. Cook fish sticks on a baking pan according to directions then transfer them to the sprayed

9 x 13" pan so the bottom of the pan is covered (it's okay if they overlap or leave space).

3. Dump out the bag of tater tots over the meat and arrange them so the meat is covered.

4. In a bowl, mix the evaporated milk and soups. Pour evenly over the top of the tater tots.

5. Top with cheese.

6. Bake at 350 degrees uncovered for about 30 minutes.

7. Take out of the oven and let cool for a few minutes before serving.

FULLY LOADED

You'll really dig this one! This is the new addition to the cookbook and has all kinds of decadent goodness! I added this one for my son Michael, who is not a fan of ground beef in general!

1 pound turkey deli lunch meat of your choice
2 pounds frozen tater tots
Jalapeno peppers, sliced
Black olives, sliced
1 cup sour cream
Green onions
½ pound of bacon, cooked crisp
2 cups shredded cheddar cheese

1. Preheat oven to 350 degrees and spray the bottom of a 9 x 13" pan with cooking spray.
2. Cook bacon until crispy and transfer to paper towels to soak up any grease. Cut up bacon using scissors or chop on a cutting board.
3. Chop the lunchmeat and place in the bottom of the sprayed 9 x 13" pan so the bottom of the pan is covered.

4. Dump out the bag of tater tots over the meat.

5. Place remaining ingredients, including bacon, in the pan and stir it all up.

6. Bake at 350 degrees uncovered for about 30 minutes.

7. Take out of the oven and let cool for a few minutes before serving.

GLUTEN-FREE

I never quite understood what gluten-free (GF) meant or what the purpose of being that way was until we met some kids with Celiac disease. Any hint of gluten could mean skin problems, stomach issues and even worse for them. That's when I educated myself on this a bit so I always had GF treats for them. And so I had to include a GF version of my tater tot casserole!

Soup mix

16 ounces Portabella mushrooms (or any mushroom with a hearty flavor)
1 tsp. olive oil
4 T. unsalted butter
1/2 cup gluten-free flour (try brown rice flour)
2 cups chicken or vegetable stock
1 1/2 cups light cream or half & half (or 1 1/8 cups plain soymilk + 3/8 cup canola oil)
Squirt of lemon juice
White pepper to taste
Tiny pinch of nutmeg
¼ cup milk

1. Sauté mushrooms over medium-low heat in 1 tsp. of olive oil. Set the mushrooms aside once they

have released their juices.

2. In a clean skillet, melt the 4 T. of butter. Once the butter is melted, gradually add the flour to the butter while constantly whisking.

3. Once you've added all of the flour, allow the roux to cook for a few minutes while you continue to whisk it.

4. Gradually began to add the stock to the roux. Add a little bit and whisk it in before you add any more. Once you've added all of the stock begin adding the cream.

5. After adding all of the cream, bring the sauce to a simmer and let it cook for one minute. Add ¼ cup milk. Continue whisking since the sauce may continue to thicken. Add the sautéed mushrooms into the sauce, and you're done.

The rest of the casserole
2 tsp. minced garlic
¼ cup milk
1 yellow bell pepper, chopped
1 ½ pounds ground beef
2 pounds frozen tater tots
½ large onion, chopped

2 cups shredded cheddar cheese

1. Preheat oven to 350 degrees and spray the bottom of a 9 x 13" pan with gluten-free cooking spray.

2. In a skillet, cook ground beef on medium heat until brown. Drain the fat and put meat back in skillet.

3. Mix in onion and pepper until cooked through. Add garlic and cook another minute.

4. Place meat mixture in bottom of sprayed 9 x 13" pan.

5. Dump out the bag of tater tots over the meat and arrange them so the meat is covered.

6. Pour soup/milk evenly over the top of the tater tots.

7. Top with cheese.

8. Bake at 350 degrees uncovered for about 30 minutes.

9. Take out of the oven and let cool for a few minutes before serving.

* Read the label on the tater tots before you buy

them. Most are already gluten-free, but of course you will want to check!

GREEN BEAN WITH FRENCH FRIED ONIONS

Growing up in the '70s, this was a staple dish at any potluck and at any family holiday meal. You get your vegetable thrown into the casserole for good measure and healthy benefits and then a nice, crunchy topping for some extra fun!

1 ½ pounds ground beef
2 pounds frozen tater tots
2 15-ounce cans green beans
1 1/3 cups French-fried onions, divided
1 12-ounce can evaporated milk
2 10.5-ounce cans cream of mushroom soup
2 cups shredded cheddar cheese

1. Preheat oven to 350 degrees and spray the bottom of a 9 x 13" pan with cooking spray.

2. In a skillet, cook ground beef on medium heat until brown. Drain the fat and put in bottom of the sprayed 9 x 13" pan.

3. Mix in about ½ of the French fried onions.

4. Dump out the bag of tater tots over the meat and arrange them so the meat is covered.

5. In a bowl, mix the evaporated milk and soups. Pour evenly over the top of the tater tots.

6. Top with cheese.

7. Bake at 350 degrees uncovered for about 25 minutes.

8. Put on the remaining onions and bake for another 5 minutes.

9. Take out of the oven and let cool for a few minutes before serving.

HAM

I'm still waiting for this dish to become a must-have at family Christmas dinners. In the meantime, I just make it when I have leftover ham steak or even ham deli meat. The cream of broccoli and mozzarella cheese make it shine!

3 cups diced, cooked ham
2 pounds frozen tater tots
1 10.5-ounce can cream of broccoli soup
1 10.5-ounce can cheddar cheese soup
1 cup shredded cheddar cheese
1 12-ounce can evaporated milk
1 cup shredded mozzarella cheese

1. Preheat oven to 350 degrees and spray the bottom of a 9 x 13" pan with cooking spray.
2. Place cooked, diced ham in bottom of the sprayed 9 x 13" pan.
3. Dump out the bag of tater tots over the meat and arrange them so the meat is covered.
4. In a bowl, mix the evaporated milk and soups. Pour evenly over the top of the tater tots.
5. Top with cheese.

6. Bake at 350 degrees uncovered for about 30 minutes.

7. Take out of the oven and let cool for a few minutes before serving.

HOT DOG

Most kids love hot dogs, and adults don't usually mind them either! So one day I decided to dice up a bunch of hot dogs and whip up a tater tot casserole with them in a quick and simple way when I had nothing else meaty in the house. The result was tasty, and everyone can top their own however they like!

8-10 hot dogs, diced
2 pounds frozen tater tots
1 12-ounce can evaporated milk
2 cups shredded cheddar cheese
2 10.5-ounce cans cream of mushroom soup
Ketchup, mustard, relish, and sauerkraut

1. Preheat oven to 350 degrees and spray the bottom of a 9 x 13" pan with cooking spray.
2. Dice hot dogs into small pieces (we don't want little kids choking!) and toss them into the bottom of the sprayed 9 x 13" pan.
3. In a bowl, mix the evaporated milk and soups. Pour evenly over the top of the hot dogs.

4. Dump out the bag of tater tots over the hot dog mixture and arrange them so the mixture is covered.

5. Top with cheese.

6. Bake at 350 degrees uncovered for about 30 minutes.

7. Take out of the oven and let cool for a few minutes before serving.

8. Serve with ketchup, mustard, relish and sauerkraut if you are adventurous!

ITALIAN

We love Italian food in my house and had to find a way to make it a tater tot casserole. Italian sausage, spaghetti sauce and mozzarella and you have a fabulous 4-ingredient meal that's as yummy as it is easy.

2 pounds Italian sausage
2 pounds frozen tater tots
1 24-ounce jar spaghetti sauce*
2 cups shredded mozzarella cheese

1. Preheat oven to 350 degrees and spray the bottom of a 9 x 13" pan with cooking spray.
2. In a skillet, cook sausage on medium heat until brown. Drain any fat and put meat in bottom of sprayed 9 x 13" pan.
3. Add jar of spaghetti sauce to sausage and stir.
4. Dump out the bag of tater tots over the meat and arrange them so the meat mixture is covered.
5. Top with cheese.

6. Bake at 350 degrees uncovered for about 30 minutes.

7. Take out of the oven and let cool for a few minutes before serving.

*we like Classico tomato and basil, unless you can get your hands on some of Kerrie's husband's homemade spaghetti sauce!

McTot Baby

If you can find the mini tater tots or the smooshed flat ones, grab a bag and make this recipe. Had to have a recipe in this cookbook to pay homage to all the babies we've had ☺

1 ½ pounds ground beef
Onion powder/garlic salt
2 pounds frozen mini tater tots
1 10.5-ounce can cream of chicken soup
1 10.5-ounce can cheddar cheese soup
1 12-ounce can evaporated milk
1 cup shredded cheddar cheese
1 cup shredded mozzarella cheese

1. Preheat oven to 350 degrees and spray the bottom of a 9 x 13" pan with cooking spray.

2. In a skillet, cook ground beef on medium heat until brown. Drain the fat and put meat back in skillet.

3. Mix in onion powder and garlic salt, then put mixture in the bottom of the sprayed 9 x 13" pan.

4. Dump out the bag of mini tater tots over the meat and arrange them so the meat is covered.

5. In a bowl, mix the evaporated milk and soups. Pour evenly over the top of the tater tots.

6. Top with cheese.

7. Bake at 350 degrees uncovered for about 30 minutes.

8. Take out of the oven and let cool for a few minutes before serving.

MEXICAN

Don't even get me started on how much I love Mexican food. I think I could live on tacos day in and day out for years! This recipe, which uses ingredients like black olives, enchilada sauce, and Rotel tomatoes, makes a spicy and yummy dish. I suggest leaving out the Rotel or making it a can of mild if you're feeding small kids!

1 pound ground beef
½ cup chopped onion
Salt, pepper, garlic powder
1 10-ounce can enchilada sauce
1 small can sliced black olives
1 10-ounce can mild Rotel tomatoes
1 can whole kernel corn, drained
2 pounds frozen tater tots
2 cups shredded cheddar cheese

1. Preheat oven to 350 degrees and spray the bottom of a 9 x 13" pan with cooking spray.
2. In a skillet, cook ground beef and onion on medium heat until meat is brown. Drain the fat and put meat back in skillet.

3. Mix in salt, pepper and garlic powder to taste, then put mixture in the bottom of the sprayed 9 x 13" pan.

4. Mix in sauce, olives, corn and Rotel.

5. Dump out the bag of tater tots over the meat and arrange them so the meat is covered.

6. Top with cheese.

7. Bake at 350 degrees uncovered for about 30 minutes.

8. Take out of the oven and let cool for a few minutes before serving.

PIZZA

Pizza is pretty much the all-American meal. It's quick and easy and pretty cheap and most everyone loves it in some form or another. Pepperoni, mushrooms, and pizza sauce are just a few of the ingredients you'll find in this totally different tater tot casserole.

1 ½ pounds ground beef
1 small onion, chopped
1 small can sliced mushrooms
1 15-ounce can or jar pizza sauce
50 slices of pepperoni, turkey or regular
2 pounds frozen tater tots
2 cups shredded mozzarella cheese
1 cup shredded cheddar cheese

1. Preheat oven to 350 degrees and spray the bottom of a 9 x 13" pan with cooking spray.
2. In a skillet, cook ground beef, onion and mushrooms on medium heat until beef is brown. Drain the fat and put mixture in the sprayed 9 x 13" pan.
3. Add pizza sauce and pepperoni and stir.
4. Top with mozzarella cheese.

5. Dump out the bag of tater tots over the meat and arrange them so the meat is covered.

6. Bake at 350 degrees uncovered for about 30 minutes.

7. Top with cheddar cheese and bake 5 minutes longer.

8. Take out of the oven and let cool for a few minutes before serving.

SAUSAGE

One day I found myself out of my stockpile of ground beef from our huge commercial freezer in the basement. I did, however, find a lot of pork sausage because my husband buys it from a guy at work who raises pigs. I used sausage and cheddar cheese soup for something different and came up with a new tater tot casserole concoction! Enjoy!

1 ½ pounds ground sausage
2 pounds frozen tater tots
1 12-ounce can evaporated milk
2 10.5-ounce cans cheddar cheese soup
1 cup shredded cheddar cheese
1 cup shredded mozzarella cheese

1. Preheat oven to 350 degrees and spray the bottom of a 9 x 13" pan with cooking spray.

2. In a skillet, cook sausage on medium heat until brown. Drain the fat and put sausage in the sprayed 9 x 13" pan.

3. Dump out the bag of tater tots over the meat and arrange them so the meat is covered.

4. In a bowl, mix the evaporated milk and soups. Pour evenly over the top of the tater tots.

5. Top with cheese.

6. Bake at 350 degrees uncovered for about 30 minutes.

7. Take out of the oven and let cool for a few minutes before serving.

SEAFOOD

We are insane for seafood at my house. You mention the word "shrimp" and it sends my kids into a tizzy. We usually only have it for very special occasions, like New Year's Eve or a special birthday, and we also only whip up this tater tot casserole for special occasions. Cream of shrimp soup can be hard to find so feel free to substitute cream of chicken for a still-great result!

1 pound fresh shrimp
½ pound fresh scallops
1 6-ounce can crabmeat
2 T. minced garlic; olive oil
2 pounds frozen tater tots
1 12-ounce can evaporated milk
2 10.5-ounce cans cream of shrimp soup
1 cup shredded cheddar cheese
1 cup shredded mozzarella cheese

1. Preheat oven to 350 degrees and spray the bottom of a 9 x 13" pan with cooking spray.

2. Put about 2 T. olive oil in a skillet and cook garlic, shrimp and scallops on medium heat until shrimp is pink and scallops are heated through.

3. Place shrimp and scallops in bottom of the sprayed 9 x 13" pan.

4. Stir in crab meat.

5. Dump out the bag of tater tots over the meat and arrange them so the meat is covered.

6. In a bowl, mix the evaporated milk and soups. Pour evenly over the top of the tater tots.

7. Top with cheese.

8. Bake at 350 degrees uncovered for about 30 minutes.

9. Take out of the oven and let cool for a few minutes before serving.

SHEPHERD'S

My mom used to make the best Shepherd's Pie when I was growing up and I would recreate it from time to time in my own way when I had a family of my own. Then, of course, I had to figure out how to turn it into a tater tot casserole and here you go with a super rockin' comfort food which basically just substitutes the tater tots for mashed potatoes!

1 ½ pounds ground beef
2 15-ounce jars brown gravy
1 15-ounce can peas
1 15-ounce can whole kernel corn
2 pounds frozen tater tots
1 cup shredded cheddar cheese

1. Preheat oven to 350 degrees and spray the bottom of a 9 x 13" pan with cooking spray.
2. In a skillet, cook ground beef on medium heat until brown. Drain the fat and put meat in bottom of the sprayed 9 x 13" pan.
3. Pour one jar of gravy on top of meat and mix.
4. Add peas and corn to beef/gravy mixture.

5. Dump out the bag of tater tots over the meat and arrange them so the meat is covered.

6. Pour the other jar of gravy evenly over the top of the tater tots.

7. Top with cheese.

8. Bake at 350 degrees uncovered for about 30 minutes.

9. Take out of the oven and let cool for a few minutes before serving.

Skinny

Sometimes you need to lighten up on a meal because you're watching calories or fat in your diet, and that's where this skinny version comes in. Made with white turkey, fat-free soup and light cheese, you still get to enjoy your comfort food ... just a little healthier!

1 ½ pounds ground white turkey
Salt and pepper to taste
Any veggies you like
1 1/2 pounds frozen tater tots
½ cup skim milk
2 10.5-ounce cans 98% fat-free cream of mushroom soup
1 cup low-fat shredded cheddar cheese

1. Preheat oven to 350 degrees and spray the bottom of a 9 x 13" pan with cooking spray.

2. In a skillet, cook ground beef on medium heat until brown. Drain the fat and put meat back in skillet.

3. Salt and pepper your meat or use any flavorings that float your boat.

4. Add any veggies that you love.

5. Add meat/veggie mixture to the sprayed 9 x 13" pan.

6. Dump out the bag of tater tots over the meat and arrange them so the meat is covered.

7. In a bowl, mix the evaporated milk and soups. Pour evenly over the top of the tater tots.

8. Top with cheese.

9. Bake at 350 degrees uncovered for about 30 minutes.

10. Take out of the oven and let cool for a few minutes before serving.

SLOPPY JOE

Kids and adults love Sloppy Joes! Take out the evaporated milk and soups and replace them with Sloppy Joe sauce (store bought or homemade) and you have a dinner that will please everyone!

1 ½ pounds ground beef
Chopped onions
1 26.5-oz. can Sloppy Joe sauce
2 pounds frozen tater tots
1 cup shredded cheddar cheese

1. Preheat oven to 350 degrees and spray the bottom of a 9 x 13" pan with cooking spray.
2. In a skillet, cook ground beef on medium heat until brown. Drain the fat and put meat back in skillet.
3. Add Sloppy Joe sauce to meat mixture, stir, then put in the sprayed 9 x 13" pan.
4. Dump out the bag of tater tots over the meat and arrange them so the meat is covered.
5. Top with cheese and onions.

6. Bake at 350 degrees uncovered for about 30 minutes.

7. Take out of the oven and let cool for a few minutes before serving.

STRING CHEESE

We had a lot of fun coming up with this recipe. We changed around a lot of things in the basic tater tot casserole recipe to come up with some of the other recipes when we asked each other, "What if we changed the type of cheese to something kids love?" String cheese! Feel free to substitute the cream of broccoli soup for something more pleasing to your family, if you like!

1 ½ pounds ground beef
Onion powder, garlic salt
12 pieces string cheese, halved
2 pounds frozen tater tots
1 12-ounce can evaporated milk
1 10.5-ounce can cream of chicken soup
1 10.5-ounce can cream of broccoli soup
1 cup shredded mozzarella cheese

1. Preheat oven to 350 degrees and spray the bottom of a 9 x 13" pan with cooking spray.

2. In a skillet, cook ground beef on medium heat until brown. Drain the fat and put meat back in skillet.

3. Mix in onion powder and garlic salt to taste, then put mixture in the bottom of the sprayed 9 x 13" pan.

4. Lay string cheese on top of meat mixture.

5. Dump out the bag of tater tots over the meat and arrange them so the meat is covered.

6. In a bowl, mix the evaporated milk and soups. Pour evenly over the top of the tater tots.

7. Top with cheese.

8. Bake at 350 degrees uncovered for about 30 minutes.

9. Take out of the oven and let cool for a few minutes before serving.

TRIPLE CHEESE

I am of the opinion that you can never have enough cheese (unless you are lactose intolerant, of course, and then you need to see the Dairy-Free recipe). As our friend Julia says, "Choose Cheese!"

1 ½ pounds ground beef
2 tsp. garlic salt
2 tsp. onion powder
2 pounds frozen tater tots
1 12-ounce can evaporated milk
1 10.5-ounce can cream of chicken soup
1 10.5-ounce can cheddar cheese soup
1 cup Monterey Jack cheese
1 cup shredded cheddar cheese
1 cup shredded mozzarella cheese

1. Preheat oven to 350 degrees and spray the bottom of a 9 x 13" pan with cooking spray.

2. In a skillet, cook ground beef on medium heat until brown. Drain the fat and put meat back in skillet.

3. Mix in onion powder and garlic salt, then put mixture in the bottom of the sprayed 9 x 13" pan.

4. Dump out the bag of tater tots over the meat and arrange them so the meat is covered.

5. In a bowl, mix the evaporated milk and soups. Pour evenly over the top of the tater tots.

6. Top with cheese.

7. Bake at 350 degrees uncovered for about 30 minutes.

8. Take out of the oven and let cool for a few minutes before serving.

TUNA

Okay, hear me out on this one. My mom used to make the best tuna casserole when I was growing up and she'd top it with crushed potato chips. That's why I tried to recreate it in a tater tot casserole recipe here! Cheese soup, tuna, peas, mushrooms and crushed chips turn this meal into something interesting and yummy!

2 pounds frozen tater tots
1 15-ounce can peas
3 cans tuna, drained
½ onion, diced
1 cup sliced mushrooms
1 10.5-ounce can Fiesta Nacho Cheese soup
1 cup milk
2 cups shredded cheddar cheese
1 cup plain potato chips, crushed

1. Preheat oven to 350 degrees and spray the bottom of a 9 x 13" pan with cooking spray.
2. Dump out the bag of tater tots into the sprayed 9 x 13" pan and make sure the bottom of the pan is covered.

3. In a bowl, mix the tuna, soup, milk, veggies and 1 cup cheese. Pour evenly over the top of the tater tots.

4. Cover with rest of the cheese and smashed up chips.

5. Bake at 350 degrees covered with foil for about 30 minutes.

6. Take out of the oven and let cool for a few minutes before serving.

TURKEY

Missing Thanksgiving? Give this recipe a try! Made with leftover or just-made turkey or even deli turkey meat, add the corn, the turkey gravy and let the tots act like mashed potatoes and you have a meal to be thankful for! I also named this for my son Samuel, because he's such a cute little turkey!

2 cups diced turkey
1 15-ounce jar turkey gravy
1 15-ounce can whole kernel corn
2 pounds frozen tater tots
2 cups shredded cheddar cheese

1. Preheat oven to 350 degrees and spray the bottom of a 9 x 13" pan with cooking spray.
2. Put turkey in bottom of the sprayed 9 x 13" pan and stir in gravy and corn.
3. Dump out the bag of tater tots over the meat and arrange them so the meat is covered.
4. Top with cheese.
5. Bake at 350 degrees uncovered for about 30 minutes.

6. Take out of the oven and let cool for a few minutes before serving.

VEGETARIAN

Although it would be pretty difficult to be one myself, I do respect my vegetarian friends and wanted to make sure I got a recipe in here for them! All I know is they look AMAZING! There's something about not eating meat that does something really cool to your skin and gives a definite healthy glow!

1 can corn, drained
1 15-ounce can green beans, drained
1 15-ounce can Northern beans, drained
Onion/garlic powder to taste
2 pounds frozen tater tots
2 10.5-ounce cans cream of celery soup
1 12-ounce can evaporated milk
2 cups shredded cheddar cheese

1. Preheat oven to 350 degrees and spray the bottom of a 9 x 13" pan with cooking spray.

2. Pour corn, green beans and Northern beans (or your favorite veggies) into bottom of the sprayed 9 x 13" pan and sprinkle with onion/garlic powder.

3. Dump out the bag of tater tots over the meat and arrange them so the meat is covered.

4. In a bowl, mix the evaporated milk and soups. Pour evenly over the top of the tater tots.

5. Top with cheese.

6. Bake at 350 degrees uncovered for about 30 minutes.

7. Take out of the oven and let cool for a few minutes before serving.

BAKER'S DOZEN DESSERTS

Dessert is a huge thing in my house, and I wanted to share 13 of our very favorites as a bonus for my readers. I hope you love them as much as we do!

ANA'S PEANUT BUTTER FUDGE (GLUTEN-FREE)

This recipe is gluten-free and comes from our sweet neighbor Ana, who loves to bake and is quite talented at it as well! If you are making this for someone with Celiac, please open a brand-new jar of peanut butter to avoid cross-contamination with any wheat products.

2 cups powdered sugar
1 cup peanut butter
½ cup melted butter
2 c. melted chocolate chips, if you like

1. Mix all ingredients except chocolate chips together in medium bowl.
2. Spread in an 8 x 8" pan.
3. Cool until firm.
4. Add melted chocolate to the top if you like, then refrigerate longer.

*Ana says: You have lots of options here. You can half-melt the chocolate chips and stir them in. You can also mix in unmelted chocolate chips to the mixture if you want a chunkier fudge. You can also use mini chocolate chips.

GRANDMA SOLSBERG'S EASY BROWNIES

My Grandma Solsberg is one of my favorite people in the world! I grew up spending a week at a time at her house in the summertime and any weekends I could. She is an amazing cook and all-around sweet person!

1 cup sugar
1 stick butter or margarine
2 eggs
¾ cup flour
3 T. cocoa

1. Preheat oven to 375 degrees and spray the bottom of an 8 x 8" baking pan with cooking spray.

2. In a bowl, mix sugar and eggs; blend in cocoa.

3. Stir flour into sugar mixture.

4. Slowly add melted butter and mix.

5. Pour batter into baking pan and bake for 25-30 minutes.

6. Remove from oven when toothpick comes out clean.

Grandma Stump's 4-Legged Dessert

My Grandma Stump is yet another super important person in my life. I remember staying a week at a time at her house and waking up to the sound of what I thought was the Easter Bunny when it was really my grandma in her slippers! She makes this 4-layered dessert but we gave it the jokey name of 4-legged!

1 cup flour
½ cup nuts, chopped
½ cup margarine, softened
8 ounces cream cheese
1 cup powdered sugar
1 8-ounce container whipped topping, divided
1 3 ½-ounce package instant chocolate pudding
3 cups milk
Toasted coconut for sprinkling (optional)

1. Preheat oven to 350 degrees.

2. Combine flour, nuts, and margarine.

3. Press mixture into a 9 x 13" pan then bake 10-15 minutes.

4. While the "crust" is cooling, mix together cream cheese, powdered sugar, and 1 cup whipped topping, then spread over top of "crust."

5. Mix pudding and milk and pour on top of previous layers.

6. Chill for a couple of hours.

7. Remove from fridge and top with remaining whipped topping.

8. Sprinkle with toasted coconut if you wish.

HEAVENLY SINFUL BARS

I like to bake these and give them as Christmas goodies or give them all year long! Then I bake a batch just for me and the kids and snack on them out of the fridge (they are better cold) until I get a sugar headache! They rock! "Only" 200 calories and 11 grams of fat per bar!

½ cup butter (1 stick)
1 brick graham crackers (about 1 ½ cups crushed)
1 14-ounce can sweetened condensed milk
1 cup chocolate chips
1 cup butterscotch chips, peanut butter chips or
   white chocolate chips (or some of each!)
½ cup shredded coconut

1. Preheat oven to 350 degrees.

2. Melt the butter and pour it into a 9 x 13" baking pan.

3. Sprinkle the graham cracker crumbs over the melted butter and mix it all up in the pan. Then pat it down flat.

4. Pour the milk as evenly as you can over the crumbs.

5. Sprinkle on the chips and coconut. You can add nuts if you like them.

6. Press it all down with a spatula.

7. Bake 20 minutes or until golden brown on top.

8. Cool for half an hour then cut into bars.

*These are AMAZING served cold!

JEN'S MOCK APPLE PIE

This yum comes from Jen, a fellow mom I met on Facebook. We started talking on the back end of Facebook and became friends, bonding over Jamberry and Younique and how we love being moms!

For the Crust
2 unbaked pie crusts
1 egg
1 T. milk
1 T. sugar

For the Filling
2 cups sugar
1 3/4 cups water
2 tsp. cream of tartar
Zest and 2 T. juice from 1 lemon
2 tsp. of vanilla extract
36 Ritz crackers, coarsely broken
2 T. unsalted butter, cut into small pieces
3/4 tsp. ground cinnamon

1. Preheat oven to 425°F.

2. In a medium saucepan combine sugar, water, and cream of tartar, whisking until sugar has dissolved. Bring mixture to boil over high heat,

whisking occasionally, then reduce heat to medium.

3. Simmer for 15 minutes or until mixture has reduced to 1 1/2 cups. Stir in zest, juice and vanilla. Set aside to cool for 30 minutes.

4. Roll out crusts. For a 9-inch pan, your bottom crust should be around 11 inches in diameter, and your top crust should be about 10 inches.

5. Place bottom crust in pie pan or dish. Add crumbled crackers. Pour syrup over crackers and dot with pieces of butter then sprinkle evenly with cinnamon.

6. Beat together egg and milk.

7. Place top crust over pie. Seal and flute the edges and brush with egg wash then sprinkle with sugar. Cut several small slits into the top crust to vent the steam.

8. Bake for 30 minutes or until golden brown.

9. Cool and serve. Store covered.

JORDAN'S GRANOLA BARS

I'm calling these Jordan's Granola Bars in honor of our favorite babysitter of all time! I like to make these when we are going on vacation or are going to be out several days during the week, gone to places such as the zoo or a local kid's farmstead.

2 cups oats
1 beaten egg
¾ cup packed brown sugar
½ cup butter
¾ tsp. cinnamon
2 tsp. vanilla extract
1 cup wheat or white flour
½ cup chopped almonds
¾ tsp. salt
1 cup mini chocolate chips
½ cup honey
½ cup wheat germ

1. Preheat oven to 350 degrees and spray the bottom of a large jelly roll pan (like a big cookie sheet with sides).
2. Mix together all ingredients in a large bowl.

3. Pour mixture onto baking pan and mash down until the entire pan is covered with the mixture. Try using wax paper or your fingers coated with cooking spray; this takes a little while!

4. Bake 20 minutes and cut while still warm or these are a nightmare to get off the pan!

JULIE'S CHOCOLATE SUICIDE

My friend Julie told me about this when we were in the thick of new motherhood and it really helped take the edge off of the stressful days since I'm not a drinker or a smoker. These days, my kids beg me to make this and it disappears fast!

1 box Devil's food cake mix
3 eggs
Oil (depends on cake mix you use)
Water
1 bag of chocolate chips
1 1/3 cups heavy cream
4 T. butter

1. Preheat oven to 350 degrees and spray the bottom of a 9 x 13" pan.

2. Bake cake according to directions on box, then let it cool completely.

3. Place chocolate chips in a medium bowl.

4. In medium saucepan, heat cream and butter until mixture is hot.

5. Pour cream/butter (ganache) over chocolate chips and let stand for 30 seconds, then whisk until smooth. Let cool 15-20 minutes.

6. In a larger bowl, crumble the cooled cake.

7. Add half the ganache mixture to the cake crumbles and mix until it resembles fudge.

8. Place ganache/cake mixture into 9 x 13" cake pan, press down, and freeze for one hour.

9. Remove cake from freezer and top with remaining ganache.

KERRIE'S KOOKIES

This is my favorite cookie recipe of all time and I don't make it often because I would weigh about 500 pounds if I did! It pretty much has everything amazing a cookie should contain!

1 ¼ cups packed brown sugar
½ cup softened butter
½ cup sugar
3 eggs
1 tsp. vanilla extract
2 tsp. baking soda
1 12-ounce jar peanut butter
4 cups quick cooking oats
1 1/3 cups chocolate chips
1 1/3 cups M&Ms

1. Preheat oven to 350 degrees.
2. Mix butter and sugars together.
3. Add eggs, vanilla, and baking soda and stir.
4. Stir in peanut butter, then oats.
5. Mix in chocolate chips and M&Ms.
6. Drop cookies by large spoonful about 2 inches apart on an ungreased baking sheet and bake 15 minutes.

7. Remove cookies from baking sheet immediately and place on wax paper.

KITTY'S ANGEL FOOD DREAM CAKE

Kitty is the sister of my friend Shannon and we hit if off immediately chatting on private message on Facebook. She is the super sweet mom of many who volunteered this recipe for the cookbook, and we love her for it!

1 3 ½-ounce package of instant vanilla pudding
1 20-ounce can crushed pineapple
1 pre-made angel food cake
1 cup whipped topping
Strawberries to decorate

1. In a bowl, mix dry vanilla pudding mix with canned pineapple, including juice.
2. Place in refrigerator for 5 minutes.
3. Remove mixture from fridge and add whipped topping. Blend gently then return to fridge.
4. Slice angel food cake in thirds horizontally.
5. Divide pudding mixture in thirds and fill the two layers.
6. Place top on and frost with remaining pudding

(top only).

7. Decorate top with sliced or whole strawberries.

8. Chill cake until ready to serve.

**You can substitute low-fat or sugar-free items.

NANA'S NO BAKE COOKIES

My stepmom is an amazing cook and is always coming up with new ideas from all sorts of places. This recipe isn't something she has made for me, but I like the alliteration of Nana and No Bake, so there you go! This is also a gluten-free recipe as long as you open a brand-new jar of peanut butter to avoid cross-contamination!

½ cup milk
2 cups sugar
3 T. cocoa
½ cup butter (1 stick)
1 tsp. vanilla extract
½ cup peanut butter
3 cups quick cooking oats

1. In a medium saucepan on high heat, add milk, sugar, butter, and cocoa.
2. Stir until mixture comes to a rolling boil. This is very important because if you don't do this, the mixture won't set up properly.
3. Take off heat and stir in peanut butter first until it's melted.

4. Then add vanilla, then the oats.

5. Scoop tablespoon-sized portions onto wax paper and let set up for a few minutes before enjoying.

NICKI'S CHERRY DUMP CAKE

This recipe is courtesy of my proofreading friend who I met on Fiverr and she is just a peach! This cherry dump cake recipe rocks my world because I love cherries and I love easy. This one's a keeper!

15-ounce can crushed pineapple
21-ounce can cherry pie filling
1 box yellow or white cake mix
1 stick of butter at room temperature

1. Preheat oven to 350 degrees.
2. Spread can of crushed pineapple and can of cherry pie filling in the bottom of a 9 x 13" pan.
3. Mix the box of cake mix with stick of butter until crumbly and sprinkle in pan on top of fruit.
4. Bake at 350 degrees for about 30 minutes.
5. Remove from oven and enjoy warm or cold!

*You might also consider putting some whipped topping on it as well … or vanilla ice cream!

ROXI'S BLUEBERRY BANANA PIE

I met Roxi in a local homeschool group and we quickly became friends. A few years ago when I got too busy with proofreading jobs on Fiverr, she really helped me out of a bind by taking on some of my work! Thanks for sending this recipe, Roxi!

2 9-inch pie shells, baked
1 8-ounce brick cream cheese
1 ¼ cup sugar
1 tsp. vanilla
21-ounce can blueberry pie filling
5 medium bananas
½ cup lemon juice
1 8-ounce tub whipped topping

1. Prepare pie crust with a fork to prevent bubbling.
2. Beat cream cheese until smooth then add sugar and vanilla and mix it all up. Fold in the whipped topping.
3. Slice bananas and dip each slice into lemon juice to prevent browning and then place half of the bananas in pie pans.

4. Put cream cheese mixture over bananas, then put another layer of bananas on top of that.

5. Spoon ½ can of blueberry pie filling on top of each pie.

6. Chill and serve!

TUTU'S CHOCOLATE STARS

My mom used to always have a bag of Brach's chocolate stars around before the recipe was changed and they weren't so good anymore. We would enjoy some while watching soap operas in the summer and Dallas and Dynasty during weeknights!

Bag of chocolate melts from a quality baking store
Plastic mold of 12 stars (get at baking store or on
 eBay or Amazon)

1. Melt 1 cup of chocolate melts in a double boiler, stirring often.*

2. Spoon chocolate into mold.

3. Lightly bang the mold on the counter to get the chocolate to settle into the cracks of the stars.

4. Put mold in refrigerator for just a few minutes.

5. Take mold out of refrigerator and pop the set-up stars onto a plate to enjoy or wrap them in pretty cellophane bags to give as gifts!

6. Repeat.

* I don't have a double boiler so I heat water in a medium pan and melt the chocolate in a smaller pan above it.

ABOUT THE AUTHORS

Jordan McGarrigle, 15 years old when this book was written (18 years old now and heading to college soon!) and the second oldest of seven tots, started out as a Mother's Helper to the McLoughlin family and instead became like a member of the family and the best go-to babysitter EVER (a.k.a. "daughtersitter"). In her spare time, she has been known to work at a veterinarian's office, play the piccolo, the flute, and volleyball. She is also quite talented at makeup application and driving her stick-shift Mustang, which she is kind enough to let Kerrie drive sometimes.

Kerrie McLoughlin, homeschooling mom to five little tots and wife to one big tot, is 44 years old and an only tot. As a freelance writer who has been published in over 150 magazines, she has also self-published several ebooks on Amazon, including *Make Money Writing About Your Kids*. Follow her on Twitter (@mommykerrie), then chase her down at The Kerrie Show, Catholic Hippie Mom or on Pinterest as mommykerrie! On Instagram she is KerrieChaos. And if you are interested in saving money or following her penny-pinching journey, check out FrugaliciousFamilyFun.com.

THANK YOU!

I want to thank you for checking out my book. There are bazillions of cookbooks out there, and I am grateful that you chose mine to read and hopefully enjoy some recipes from. I truly hope you enjoyed cooking the tater tot recipes and making the dessert recipes! I know my family loves them!

If you enjoyed *The Tater Tot Casserole Cookbook*, I would love your help and support! If you would please take a moment to head to Amazon and leave me a review for this book, I would appreciate it so much! I value your feedback and it helps me to make important updates to my books. I also love when readers share my books with their family, friends, coworkers, and neighbors. It is my dream and goal to write books for people that help them make their lives easier and have more fun in the process!

I'd also love it if you'd check out my other book

offerings on Kindle and in print. I always put my books on Kindle Unlimited so if you pay your 10 bucks a month into that program like I do, you can "rent" my books for free. Just return them when you're done! You might want to consider going to my author page on Amazon and clicking "follow" so you get an email when I publish new books!

Please don't forget that if you bought the print version of this book you can get the Kindle edition (with photos!) free!

I always love to hear from readers so please contact me at mommykerrie@yahoo.com if you have any questions or comments.

Made in the USA
Coppell, TX
13 November 2019